Life is a Business and a Jungle.

I WANT TO BE A SUCCESSFUL ENTREPRENEUR

Qualities in the profile of an entrepreneur that we all want to know in order to make the decision to embark on an entrepreneurial journey

CARLOS CÁRDENAS VERDE

Cover and Collection Design: CG Publicidad Diseño y Soluciones Web
http://cgpublicidad.web.ve/

All rights reserved. Total or partial reproduction of this work, its incorporation into a computer system, or its transmission in any form or by any means (electronic, mechanical, photocopying, recording, or otherwise) without prior written permission from the copyright holder is prohibited. Infringement of these rights may constitute a crime against intellectual property.

This book is designed to provide information and motivation to our readers. It is sold with the understanding that the author does not engage in providing any form of psychological, legal, or other professional advice. The content of each chapter is solely the expression and opinion of the author. There is no express or implied warranty by the choice of the editor or the author included in any of the contents of this volume.

Neither the editor nor the individual author shall be liable for any physical, psychological, emotional, financial, or commercial damages, including, without limitation, special, incidental, consequential, or other damages.

CONTENTS

INTRODUCTION 7

CHAPTER I: Why is the World a Business and a Jungle? 11
    Why is the world a business? 11
    Why Become an Entrepreneur? 12
    Why is the world like a jungle? 15
    Do you truly desire to thrive? 16

CHAPTER II: Skills and Attitudes 21
    How to Identify Our Talents, Strengths, and Positive Aspects 23
        Figure N° 1. Model list of attributes 24
    Skills for a successful entrepreneur: 26
    Attitudes for being a successful entrepreneur: 27

CHAPTER III: Knowledge and Tools 31
    Necessary Tools 33
        Figure No. 2 Kanban Board Model 36
        Figure No. 3 SWOT Analysis Matrix Model (Strengths, Opportunities, Weaknesses, and Threats) 37

CHAPTER IV: Learning and Experience 39

CHAPTER V: The Decision 43
    How to Start a Business? 45

CONCLUSION 49

ABOUT THE AUTHOR 53

INTRODUCTION

"I Want to Be a Successful Entrepreneur" is the first book in the series "Life is a Business and a Jungle." It is aimed at individuals who aspire for more than just being an employee or earning a basic income. In recent years, job opportunities have become scarce, while the demand for greater knowledge, dedication, and often unsatisfying tasks has increased.

Every day, more people are drawn to the idea of starting their own business, hoping to generate income from a fulfilling venture that allows for a balanced personal and family life. However, many individuals postpone their dreams and eventually give up without taking the leap. It could be due to a lack of motivation, fear, or simply because they were never guided on what it takes to succeed.

It is common to come across social media posts from individuals expressing their desire to be their own boss or start their own business. While many aspire to this, few truly understand the requirements of entrepreneurship.

Entrepreneurship is a commitment to oneself and others. Most of us have been taught the traditional process: study hard, get good grades, secure a good job, and earn a high income by excelling in our field. However, being an employee does not always guarantee financial success or personal fulfillment. That's when the inner voice reminds us that we deserve more, whether in terms of income or personal satisfaction. It is at this point that we turn our attention to independence, desiring to dedicate our time and effort to something of our own that brings us both satisfaction and the financial stability we need.

The first and most crucial step is making the decision to become an entrepreneur. But how can you make a decision about something you know very little about? We often lack knowledge and guidance on what is needed and how to get started. This is precisely what "THE BEGINNING," the focus of this book, aims to address.

We frequently question whether we have what it takes to run a business and whether we are ready to face the challenges that lie ahead. Throughout this book, you will have the opportunity to develop your own concept, pave your own path, and make informed decisions.

"I Want to Be a Successful Entrepreneur" is about embarking on the journey of business ownership. It starts by teaching you the essential skills and knowledge you need to acquire, but above all, it emphasizes self-discovery.

Everything begins with understanding who you truly are, not who you think you are or what others say you are. Within these pages, you will find tips and advice on how to gain a better understanding of yourself and evaluate your potential as an entrepreneur.

It's important to note that entrepreneurship is not an innate quality. If you decide to become an entrepreneur but currently lack the necessary abilities, you can study and work to acquire them because, as mentioned earlier, it ultimately depends on your decision.

Throughout this book, you will discover the aptitudes and attitudes necessary for entrepreneurial success, the knowledge and tools you should possess, and the importance of identifying what you need to learn and understand, as well as the experiences you already have, in order to make THE DECISION.

You may have many questions as you embark on this journey, but by reading this book, you will gain a clearer understanding of what it means to be an entrepreneur, what qualities you possess to enter the business world, and how you should prepare for this new adventure. Enjoy the journey!

CHAPTER I: *Why is the World a Business and a Jungle?*

You might be curious about the title of this series and why it compares the world to both a business and a jungle. It may sound primitive at first, but it holds a certain charm and deeper meaning. I don't want to instill fear in you, making you believe that starting a business is a life-or-death struggle or that you'll be devoured by stronger competitors. My intention is to encourage you to see the world of business from a broader perspective, beyond just the pursuit of monetary gain or the survival challenges faced in a competitive environment.

Why is the world a business?

A business is the integration of various resources (material, financial, human, intellectual, and time) with the purpose of satisfying a need and generating profits. In simpler terms, it is the establishment of an entity that has enough independence to sustain itself economically and provide benefits to its owners. The motivation behind starting a business lies in developing an idea that addresses a need in a different and innovative way, creating job opportunities, and yielding favorable returns for the owners.

Viewing the world as a business involves considering multiple elements such as ideas, innovation, efficiency, resources, profitability, meeting needs, mission, and vision. By the end of this chapter, we will clarify how we will be using these terms throughout the book.

There are numerous approaches and pathways to starting any type of business because, as we will explore later, there are countless possibilities and sectors to engage with. You simply need to make the decision and choose the option that aligns best with your interests and goals.

Why Become an Entrepreneur?

The decision to become an entrepreneur is driven by various factors that are unique to each individual. It depends on personal motivations and the opportunities that arise at a given moment. However, becoming an entrepreneur is not merely a matter of chance; it requires preparation and having the vision to recognize opportunities that others may overlook.

So why choose entrepreneurship? Why start your own venture instead of working for someone else? According to the United Nations Development Coordination Office (UNDCO) and the International Labor Organization (ILO), the unemployment rate in Latin America reached 8% in 2019, the highest it has been in the past 10 years. In an environment of slower economic growth in the region, finding an ideal job that meets your economic demands, professional aspirations, personal circumstances, and offers a pleasant work environment is increasingly challenging. This is especially true if you've read books on financial freedom that discuss the concept of not relying on a fixed salary and the pursuit of generating passive income, which is income earned without active involvement in its production. Moreover, social media platforms are filled with viral posts showcasing business ideas and motivational content encouraging lucrative additional income with minimal or no capital investment.

All these factors have sparked curiosity among individuals of various age groups. Young people are inclined towards generating their own income and achieving independence, often starting with small tasks or recruiting affiliates even without capital. Professionals who desire extra income, typically within their field of expertise, explore working independently or with different clients. Finally, individuals approaching retirement age, who may have limited opportunities for job advancement or reemployment, seek to stay active or supplement their pensions, which are often insufficient. All these groups share a common motivation: the desire for more and the improvement of their future, starting now.

Whether you identify with any of the mentioned cases or not, it doesn't mean that this book is not for you. Perhaps you're waiting for a sign that says, "Hey, that's what I want." In fact, one of the main motivations behind writing this book is to motivate and guide future entrepreneurs and business owners. This initiative serves two purposes for me. First, it serves as self-advice. I write it as if it were a comment to my younger self, as during my youth, I was never focused on pursuing anything specific. I was like a surfer in the sea, occasionally catching good waves and taking advantage of them, but without thinking about the future. Needless to say, there was a lot of time that I didn't use efficiently, time that could have allowed me to acquire better skills and a better current status. While I genuinely enjoyed that stage of my life, the time has come to embrace who I am destined to be and, likewise, help you become who you are destined to be.

The second reason is the desire to assist people in making the decision to embark on entrepreneurship. I currently live in Venezuela, and as you may know, the economic and social situation here is very challenging, as it is in the rest of Latin America. There is a significant portion of the population unable to find satisfactory employment and, consequently, struggle to meet their basic needs. Furthermore, we are currently experiencing one of the most severe economic recessions the world has ever seen, which has forced us to be creative in generating income. Therefore, if you are reading this, I hope that through entrepreneurship, you can become what you have always wanted to be and experience the fulfillment you have always desired.

I don't say this merely as empty words, but because everything begins when you make the decision, take the first step, come up with your first idea to fight for, define a dream, and repeat to yourself, "This is what I want."

As you can see, achieving your dream requires a certain level of financial stability. Whether you're an artist or a tycoon, an athlete or a university student, there are still financial obligations to meet: food, housing, utilities, transportation, taxes, and contributing to charitable causes, among other things. Money is necessary, and it's important to find creative ways to earn it. But how do we do it? Where do we start?

Starting a business may seem daunting, but the first step is always the most important. It's a gradual process of growth, and you don't need to know everything all at once. While it presents challenges and requires hard work, it's not impossible to start a business. To begin, we need to introspect and consider what we want, how we want to achieve it, and what steps we'll take. This perspective reveals the world as a jungle, with opportunities waiting to be explored.

Why is the world like a jungle?

When we think of the word "jungle," some may envision the classic Disney movie "The Jungle Book"® with its wild animals, lush vegetation, predators, and prey. Or perhaps a documentary showcasing the diverse wildlife of the Amazon or Africa. While these associations capture the essence, I want to delve deeper into the concept of the jungle. It represents not only untamed wilderness but also unexplored territories waiting to be discovered. In reality, there are countless plant species, animals, and insects that remain unknown in jungles around the world. The reason for this is that few individuals dare to uncover the hidden wonders that could potentially revolutionize our understanding of the world. This could be due to the inherent risks, challenging living conditions, or simply a lack of curiosity and willingness to explore.

However, if our heart's desire lies within the metaphorical jungle, we must venture there ourselves. Many people will question our motives, cautioning us about the dangers, deeming it unnecessary, or labeling it as too risky. They may suggest pursuing an easier path and warn us that we could even face death. It can be disheartening, but as rational beings, we understand that to thrive in such an environment, preparation is essential. Not only do we need to survive, but we also want to make the most of what we seek.

In this endeavor, we recognize that our decision to embark on this journey requires determination, even if we're uncertain about the exact path we will take. We must prepare ourselves thoroughly, envisioning the possible scenarios that may arise along the way.

Do you truly desire to thrive?

Now that we have made the decision to venture into the jungle, it is imperative that we prepare ourselves accordingly. We must delve into the study of survival techniques such as water purification, hunting, and identifying edible fruits amidst the vegetation, among other essential skills. Consulting with individuals who have embarked on similar journeys before is crucial; we can learn from their experiences, challenges, and encountered problems. In short, we need to gather as much information as possible. Of course, we won't embark on this crusade alone. Assembling a team of specialists in various areas relevant to our quest is vital. We'll require tools, utensils, instruments, and provisions. To acquire these necessary resources, capital is essential. While some funds may come from our personal savings, it may also be necessary to seek external financing from an investor who sees value in our expedition. Additionally, we must not neglect the importance of familiarizing ourselves with the inhabitants of the jungle. It is an amalgamation of knowledge that we must absorb, memorize, and put into practice.

You likely foresee the direction this is heading. In today's world, being highly prepared and possessing abundant resources is vital for survival in a competitive market.

You need a clear idea, a plan encompassing medium and long-term actions, a well-defined strategy, sufficient capital, a competent team, and an abundance of courage and patience to achieve the objectives and goals we set for ourselves. We must understand how the operating environment functions and embrace its rules of engagement. So, I ask you: Are you willing to undertake all the necessary actions, make the required preparations, and transform your dream of starting your own business into a reality? I am confident your answer is a resounding "YES, I'M"

Similar to the business realm, certain terms require clarification. In our context, we need to define terms such as skill, perseverance, leadership, teamwork, and decision-making. I will provide simple, easily understandable definitions that we will refer to frequently, ensuring effective communication.

These definitions are not meant to be rigid, but rather serve as points of reference. The terms are as follows:

Benefit: It represents a positive outcome, particularly an economic gain resulting from an activity or investment.

Decision-making: It encompasses the entire process of evaluating and choosing a specific option from a universe of possibilities, employing reasoning and will, in order to resolve or carry out a particular situation or activity.

Efficiency: It pertains to the ability to achieve a desired, expected, or longed-for effect with minimal resources or within the shortest possible time.

Idea: It is a mental representation that arises spontaneously from a person's reasoning or imagination.

Innovation: It refers to the introduction of changes that bring novelty and aim to modify existing elements for improvement.

Leadership: It encompasses a set of managerial or directive skills possessed by an individual to influence the behavior or actions of people or a specific workgroup, inspiring them to work enthusiastically towards common goals and objectives.

Mission: It encompasses all actions undertaken to achieve a purpose within a specific timeframe. It can be defined as the motive, purpose, end, or reason for the existence of a company.

Perseverance: It is the unwavering and continuous determination to do something or perform it in a specific manner.

Resources: They are sources or supplies from which a benefit is derived. Resources should possess three key characteristics: usefulness, availability, and eventual consumption or depletion.

Satisfaction of a need: It involves the pursuit of fulfilling or addressing a lack of something, whether material or emotional.

<u>Skill:</u> We will define it as an individual's ability to perform a task correctly and with ease.

<u>Teamwork:</u> It comprises work carried out by several individuals, where each contributes their part, and all work towards a common objective.

<u>Vision:</u> It encompasses the goals and purposes a company sets for itself, aiming to achieve them in the future.

I understand that there may be additional terms you wish to define or comprehend their meaning. The purpose behind all this is to establish a shared language and ensure a mutual understanding of each concept.

CHAPTER II: *Skills and Attitudes*

Once the decision to embark on the entrepreneurial journey has been made, it becomes essential to assess whether you possess the qualities required to be a successful entrepreneur. This doesn't mean that being an employee is a bad thing, but often, we yearn for more in life and seek personal satisfaction or the opportunity to have something of our own. That is why, from the very beginning, it is important to introspect and closely examine your true self, identifying your personal strengths and weaknesses to determine areas that may require improvement. Let's begin by discussing Skills and Attitudes.

The topic of skills and attitudes, especially those relevant to entrepreneurs, is extensive and subjective. It is important to note that we won't delve too deeply into the psychological aspects, but rather aim to provide practical understanding for utility and comprehension purposes. Firstly, let's differentiate between these terms, as they are often confused or misunderstood. For the purpose of this book, we will define them as follows:

Skills refer to the abilities, capacities, or proficiencies that an individual possesses to perform specific activities proficiently. For instance, when we witness someone skillfully playing the piano, we can acknowledge their aptitude to excel as a pianist.

On the other hand, *attitudes* encompass the habitual behavior of an individual, their way of expressing their mood, or their reaction to different situations. Attitudes reflect their unique approach to life and how they navigate their daily existence. For example, when we receive an invitation to go out but notice dark clouds in the sky, we may decline the invitation assuming it will rain. This can be considered a negative attitude. As we can observe, skills reflect our inherent capabilities, while attitudes represent our responses and approaches to circumstances. Skills highlight our predisposition to excel in certain areas, whereas attitudes are influenced by an individual's upbringing and cultural background.

Now, what does all this lead to? Simply put, it is imperative to assess our skills and attitudes before fully immersing ourselves in entrepreneurship and assuming the role of business owners. To assist you in this process, I present a method for determining your strengths through a table that includes various aspects you consider important, such as knowledge, experiences, skills, and attitudes. I encourage you to conduct thorough research on this topic, as self-awareness and understanding your strengths are crucial for effectively addressing any potential "weaknesses."

How to Identify Our Talents, Strengths, and Positive Aspects

If your research has led you to various perspectives or unsatisfactory results, I recommend conducting the following assessment:

1. Create a list of your positive attributes: Take the time to write down all the qualities you consider to be your

strengths. For instance, "I enjoy reading," "I am a quick learner," "I have experience in customer service," "I am passionate about music," "People often seek my advice when facing challenges," and so on.

2. Categorize your list based on the following classifications (Refer to Figure 1):
   a. Knowledge (things you know): This category encompasses the information and expertise you possess. For example, proficiency in operating computers, proficiency in using word processors and spreadsheets, completion of first aid courses, etc.
   b. Experiences (things you have learned through practice): This category includes the practical skills and knowledge you have gained from past encounters. For instance, dealing with the public, driving a vehicle, managing a business, and so forth.
   c. Skills (things you do with ease or without much effort): Here, you should list the abilities and aptitudes that come naturally to you. For instance, public speaking, mathematical reasoning, verbal expression, drawing, and other skills you possess effortlessly.
   d. Attitudes (approaches to situations): This category refers to your attitudes and outlook on life. Include traits such as maintaining a positive mindset, seeking reconciliation in conflicts, taking initiative, and any other characteristics that shape your approach to various situations.

Knowledge	Experience
Skills	Attitudes

Figure N° 1. Model list of attributes

3. Validate some of your positive aspects with people close to you. Take the time to have conversations with your friends and family members, and ask them to share their observations about you. If they mention something that aligns with what you have written down, it helps to validate and confirm those qualities. Sometimes, others can offer insights and perspectives that you may have overlooked or underestimated. Add those observations to your list and consider seeking validation from multiple sources.
4. Lastly, from the list of positive aspects you have compiled, identify what activities bring you joy, satisfaction, or passion. Reflect on what truly resonates with you and what aligns with your interests and values.

Once you have a clear understanding of your strengths and weaknesses, you can define your identity and identify areas where you excel. This self-awareness is invaluable as it reinforces and highlights qualities that you may have already believed you possessed, thus boosting your self-esteem. This self-knowledge becomes particularly crucial when you embark on the path of entrepreneurship. Armed with an awareness of your positive attributes and areas for improvement, you can focus on strengthening or developing those skills, and in some cases, eliminating any excesses.

Now that you have a better understanding of yourself, we can proceed by creating a list of essential skills and attitudes that are important for a successful entrepreneur. However, it is important to note that I will focus on more general skills and attitudes, as the specific requirements may vary depending on the nature of the business. Do not consider this list as something static or universally applicable; it is subjective and open to personal interpretation. If you disagree with any of the suggestions and would like to replace them based on your existing knowledge, it is commendable to exercise your judgment and have a different perspective. This book aims to guide you and is not about providing a miraculous formula. Throughout this journey, each individual will add what they find most relevant and aspire to become.

Skills for a successful entrepreneur:

1. Problem-solving: This refers to the ability to identify, plan, and take action to solve problems effectively.

2. Leadership: It encompasses the capacity to influence the behavior and actions of individuals or a group, inspiring them to work towards predefined goals. True leadership goes beyond simply giving orders; it involves inspiring and guiding your team.
3. Flexibility: It is the ability to embrace new ideas and adapt to changing circumstances or situations. This trait can be challenging to develop as we often resist change.
4. Creativity: This skill involves generating new ideas or concepts by combining existing knowledge, leading to innovative and original solutions. It applies to both the products or services offered and the approach to daily business situations. Creativity and innovation go hand in hand.
5. Teamwork: It goes beyond leadership and involves the capability to collaborate and work harmoniously with a group of individuals to achieve specific objectives and goals in a coordinated manner. Effective communication and collaboration within the team are crucial.

Attitudes for being a successful entrepreneur:

1. Proactivity: This refers to taking the initiative to address situations or operations that require attention, as well as the ability to respond to various circumstances.
2. Self-Confidence: It is the quality that allows you to have a positive self-image, believing in your abilities and feeling capable of achieving your goals. It involves

having realistic confidence in your talents without arrogance, based on your actual capabilities.
3. Initiative: It is the willingness to independently start something or seek solutions to problems without external factors pushing you towards your objectives. It means taking action and doing what needs to be done, even if it falls outside your designated responsibilities.
4. Positivity: This attitude involves approaching situations with an optimistic mindset, always seeking the silver lining and maintaining a constructive outlook to find potential solutions.
5. Responsibility: It is the quality of committing to act correctly and with integrity, taking ownership and being accountable for the consequences of your actions.

As mentioned earlier, these skills and attitudes are not presented as rigid standards or absolute requirements. It can be beneficial to conduct surveys or gather opinions from other entrepreneurs, mentors, and advisors to understand the perspectives and reasons behind the skills and attitudes they consider important. The key is to reinforce and leverage your strengths. Skills and attitudes can be developed with focused effort. While everyone possesses innate gifts, utilizing them in your business endeavors allows you to earn money by doing what comes naturally to you, and if it's something you enjoy, even better.

However, it is crucial to have direction and determination, as you will need high levels of motivation and self-evaluation to stay on track. Envision your mission and vision close your eyes, and project a mental image of what you want to achieve. Visualize it, create a drawing, and place it somewhere visible, so you can see it every day. This practice will reinforce your goals and the path you wish to pursue.

When you have a goal or objective, you know where your efforts will lead you and how your talents will come into play. It is crucial to understand where you want or need to go and how your skills can be utilized.

For example, if you have a talent for connecting with people and persuading them to make purchases, and at the same time, you aspire to become a chef and pursue a food business because you enjoy cooking, it will take time to prepare and master the skills required for the latter option before turning it into a business.

However, if you engage in a product line where you can leverage your ability to connect with people and engage in buying and selling, you could generate income almost immediately and with minimal effort.

Hence, it is important to know your dreams and recognize what you excel at. It doesn't mean that if you have a passion for singing and are also skilled at cooking, you must abandon your singing aspirations and solely focus on becoming a culinary star. It all depends on your decision and what you believe is best for you. There are athletes who had incredible skills in their youth, which they leveraged to become successful businessmen later in life (e.g., basketball player Charles Barkley or baseball player Alex Rodriguez, for example).

No dream excludes another; it is a matter of utilizing available resources to your advantage, always remembering that you must meet the needs of others in an innovative way.

CHAPTER III: *Knowledge and Tools*

An essential characteristic that sets entrepreneurs apart is their ability to learn and be self-taught. Initially, we seek advice from people around us, looking for mentors or experts within our circle of friends who can provide insights into starting a business.

But, it is crucial to continuously seek up-to-date information to ensure that our efforts are on the right track. Therefore, we must take responsibility for our own learning by consulting multiple sources, learning from others' experiences, reading blogs and books, watching videos, participating in forums, and taking online or in-person courses. All of these activities are meant to inspire us and provide a broader perspective on the commitment we make to ourselves when starting a business.

At times, the amount of knowledge to acquire or learn may seem overwhelming, and you might feel that you don't have enough time. It's understandable. You don't need to be an expert in every financial, legal, psychological, or administrative aspect.

However, having a basic understanding is important. As entrepreneurs, we can't be knowledgeable about everything, but we can build a team that decentralizes information based on their areas of expertise. Remember that it's normal to realize how much we don't know as we continue to learn. However, surrounding ourselves with a well-trained team can help alleviate that anxiety.

Now, let's return to the topic at hand. Regardless of the business venture you wish to pursue, here are some areas of knowledge that, in my opinion, you should not overlook:

- Economics: Understanding the process of producing goods or services, distribution and consumption, and how national and international factors influence markets.
- Finance, Accounting, and Financial Management: While you don't need to be an expert, it's important to know how to manage your company's resources, classify them, and have a basic understanding of the source and destination of the funds you handle. You should be aware of whether the activities you undertake generate economic benefits and comply with the legal requirements related to your business. Every financial decision should align with commercial, tax, civil, and other applicable laws in your country.
- Marketing, Advertising, and Promotion: Having the skills necessary to sell your ideas, projects, and products to others is crucial. You need to know if your product satisfies the needs of your customers. These tools will help you identify your target market and convince potential investors to support your business.
- Personnel Management: Managing your team, providing guidance and motivation, is notably important. You should establish guidelines that allow you to set goals and objectives, develop strategies, all while aligning them with your mission and vision.

- Public Relations: Building relationships with suppliers, investors, clients, strategic allies, the community, and the media is crucial. This involves actively listening, informing, and persuading them effectively to gain support and loyalty for present and future actions. Excellent communication skills, both oral (individual and public speaking) and written, are essential.
- Technology: Being familiar with different computer tools, including hardware and software, applications, websites, social media platforms, and cloud-based services, is essential in the 21st century. Understanding these technologies will simplify various tasks in your daily routines and business operations.

It is not necessary for you to become an expert in all of these areas. You can seek support and surround yourself with professionals who are knowledgeable in each field to complement your own skills and knowledge. Remember that the key is to have a general understanding of these areas and know when and where to seek specialized assistance.

Necessary Tools

As an entrepreneur, having access to a wide range of resources is essential to ensure the smooth flow of activities in your business. Among these resources, tools play a crucial role. The necessary tools may vary depending on your level of preparation and the specific nature of your venture or business. However, it is always important to be aware of the available tools and understand why you need them.

Here are some of the most essential tools:

- Computer with an Internet connection: Your primary workstation should be equipped with a computer and an Internet connection. In the 21st century, it is almost mandatory to have these tools to carry out various tasks such as planning, record-keeping, and activity control. They enable you to send emails, access social media platforms, review your bank account, visit competitor websites, and more.
- Smartphone or Tablet: These devices are extremely useful as they keep you connected wherever you are. They allow you to access social media, emails, contact lists, activity schedules, applications, texts, and many other things without the need for a PC or laptop. They also provide the convenience of making phone calls via the internet or local calls.
- Word processor: Having a word processor, whether it's free software or licensed, is necessary for communication purposes. It allows you to write letters or official documents related to your business.
- Spreadsheets: Similar to word processors, spreadsheets can be free software or licensed. They are one of the most essential and versatile tools that every entrepreneur should learn to use. With spreadsheets, you can create various formats, control receipts, calculate payroll, manage expenses, and much more. This tool, combined with your analytical skills, can assist you with daily tasks within your company.
- Business models: A business plan is a document that outlines the objectives of your company and the strategies to achieve them. Developing a business plan

in advance is necessary to execute the attainment of objectives coherently. You can also use the Business Model Canvas, a simple method that covers nine basic aspects of any business.
- Kanban boards: This tool is very useful for task execution and is divided into three phases: To-Do, In Progress, and Done. It allows you to add activities for each person to focus on completing small tasks that contribute to achieving small objectives. (See Figure No. 2)

To Do	In Progress	Done

Figure No. 2 Kanban Board Model

- Google Tools: Email, Photos, Google Drive, and Calendars. Having access to a cloud storage solution, regardless of its size, allows you to store and back up information that can be accessed anytime, anywhere in the world.

SWOT Analysis Matrix: A simple tool that helps you assess the internal strengths and weaknesses of your business, as well as the external opportunities and threats it faces. This tool provides valuable insights into your business and enables you to make necessary corrections or gain confidence in how your venture is performing. (See Figure No. 3)

Internal Aspects	External Aspects
Strengths	Opportunities
Weaknesses	Threats

Figure No. 3 SWOT Analysis Matrix Model (Strengths, Opportunities, Weaknesses, and Threats)

- Website, Blogs, or Social Media Accounts: It's important to have an online presence through a website, blogs, or social media accounts. Being accessible through phone calls, local or internet-based messaging applications, or having a public profile on the web or social media platforms will help you reach and connect with potential clients at a lower cost and with global coverage. It's one of the most effective ways to promote yourself.

These are the essential tools you need to start your business. While it's beneficial to be familiar with and use these tools as an entrepreneur, not having them should not be an obstacle. If you lack expertise in a particular area, you can hire personnel to cover those aspects. These individuals can be either permanent employees or freelancers, depending on the duration and complexity of the tasks and the economic feasibility of hiring their services. Ultimately, the goal is to achieve maximum efficiency. Time is money, so if you don't have time to perform simple tasks, delegate them to someone else. It's not a waste of money; rather, your time spent on other activities is more valuable than engaging in routine tasks.

CHAPTER IV: *Learning and Experience*

When embarking on a new venture, it's common to feel that although we have theoretical knowledge, we lack practical experience. The fear of making mistakes or the uncertainty of the unknown can make us hesitant to take action. However, it's important to recognize that nobody is born knowing everything. Making mistakes and learning from them is a fundamental part of the entrepreneurial journey. In fact, the cost of those mistakes is an investment in gaining valuable EXPERIENCE.

There's a quote attributed to Albert Einstein that holds significant value: "*Learning is experience, the rest is just information.*" Don't be afraid to make mistakes or fail, as they provide valuable learning opportunities. As Einstein also said, "*Anyone who has never made a mistake has never tried anything new.*" It's crucial to overcome the fear of failure and take action. Each obstacle or failure is an opportunity for growth and improvement. Who wouldn't want to improve?

So, what do we mean by learning? Learning is any process that results in the acquisition or modification of skills, abilities, knowledge, or behaviors through direct experience, study, observation, reasoning, or instruction. It's a continuous process of acquiring new knowledge and adapting it for future situations. Experience, on the other hand, is the result of learning. It's how we validate and apply the knowledge we acquire through observation or action, whether through simulations or real-life situations. As we can see, learning and experience go hand in hand in any action we take. However, it's important to consider different types of experience:

a. Experience as a business owner: This refers to the experience gained in managing various aspects of your business, such as payment and collection control, personnel management, and tax obligations.
b. Experience in the specific activity of your business: This pertains to the expertise and knowledge you develop in the core operations of your business, such as being a master baker, pastry chef, or efficiently managing inventory and the production process.

It's crucial to strive for a broad knowledge base as an entrepreneur. Many experts in the business field emphasize the importance of being the architect of your own knowledge. Acquiring knowledge provides a foundation for making informed decisions. Remember, the best decision is the result of the best information available. While trial and error are part of the learning process, not everything has to be learned that way. Reading about the lives of successful businesspeople like Donald Trump, Kylie Jenner, Steve Jobs, Bill Gates, Oprah Winfrey, Mark Zuckerberg, Jeff Bezos, Jack Ma, and others can provide valuable insights and inspiration. Books are an excellent source of wisdom and experiences that can compensate for a lack of personal experience. Gradually, through the practice of your activities, you will gain experience and learn from both good and bad decisions. Reflection and introspection will be your best allies in acquiring experience.

The business world demands a wealth of knowledge and the ability to apply it effectively. It requires imagination, confidence to create something new, and the drive to excel in your chosen field. If you choose the path of entrepreneurship, make continuous learning your guiding principle. Read books, attend conventions, forums, and talks that provide not only knowledge but also connect you with experts in your field of study or specialization. Engaging with other entrepreneurs and drawing inspiration from their experiences can be invaluable.

Utilize the internet to browse entrepreneurship blogs related to your business, participate in forums, and enroll in courses. The key is to EDUCATE YOURSELF. By expanding your knowledge base, you increase your chances of finding the answers you need or knowing where and what to search for.

Mentorship is another valuable tool in your entrepreneurial journey. Seek out mentors who can provide guidance and support in the business field. There is a wealth of information available online to help you find a mentor. Additionally, building a circle of friends involved in business can be beneficial. Listen to their experiences, as they may offer valuable advice that is specifically relevant to you. You can also connect with me on my Facebook page (details will be shared at the end of the book) where daily experiences and advice are shared to support you on your entrepreneurial journey.

Creativity should also be a vital component of your experience. Challenge yourself to see things from a different and innovative perspective. Find better ways to satisfy customer needs, differentiate yourself from competitors, and evaluate the image you project with your product or service. Ultimately, you should be able to answer the question: "Why does the customer need me?" It's about transforming your ideas into compelling solutions that make customers choose you and realize they have a need they didn't even know existed. While there is ample information available online on these topics, it's up to you to find your own essence, character, and image. You will go through various stages and appreciate many qualities, but only a few will define your essence. You won't discover it unless you take the time to explore new approaches. After all, following the same path as others will not lead you to different destinations.

CHAPTER V: *The Decision*

Becoming an entrepreneur and a business owner is not a path that everyone chooses. Those who embark on this journey are fully aware of the hard work, critical thinking, development, and attention to detail it requires. There are countless variables, equations, and challenges to overcome. However, despite all of these obstacles, we yearn for it. We are willing to make sacrifices, giving up our sleep, leisure time, and distractions. Sacrifices must be made, but rewards await us. Nothing, absolutely nothing, compares to the feeling of saying, "I DID IT!" Especially when many people doubted you, telling you to give up because it seemed too difficult or unattainable. The satisfaction of achieving and realizing your dreams will transform you into a shining star and serve as an example of success for others.

It all sounds wonderful, but as I mentioned in the beginning, it all starts with the first step—making the decision to do it. Many of you may find the idea of having your own business appealing, especially if it's something you enjoy, excel at, or find easy to do. However, you may doubt whether you are capable of taking on the task. Let me reiterate: being an entrepreneur is not an innate trait. You have the power to change your destiny; you build it day by day, one step at a time. Dedicate a few hours every day to work on your business. Invest time in developing your idea. Look at yourself in the mirror and ask, "Who do I want to become?" Let's do a simple exercise: if you devote two hours every day, seven days a week, to your entrepreneurship, that would amount to nearly 60 hours per month, and 720 hours per year. That's a significant investment. While people recognize the money you invest in a business as a financial investment, only a few truly appreciate the time you dedicate to it. Money can be recovered, but time cannot. That's why, at this moment, your most important investment is your time and how you utilize it.

Entrepreneurship is not solely about money or financial security. It encompasses freedom, passion, and dreams. It's about creating, satisfying needs, and generating employment. It's about contributing to a society where the middle class is shrinking, job stability is diminishing, and relying solely on social security is inadequate. Entrepreneurship is about setting your own rules, instigating change, and experiencing the satisfaction of what you have achieved and what more you can accomplish. It's about continually doing more, positively influencing the world, and making it a better place. That is the essence of entrepreneurship—building remarkable things that future generations can benefit from.

We start off feeling scared, stepping outside of our comfort zones, seeking motivation, getting to know ourselves, and creating tools. We learn from the knowledge we acquire day by day, striving to survive. We proclaim to the world (the jungle) that we can overcome obstacles and more. Gradually, we realize our capabilities and the incredible things we can accomplish with our knowledge and who we are. Yet, we still feel that it's not enough. We become aware of our limitations and the gaps in our knowledge, so we continue to study, prepare ourselves, and train our minds for the challenges that lie ahead.

Let me ask you: Why have you chosen to embark on this journey? What motivates you? What do you aspire to achieve? What are your desires? What would you do if you attained your lifelong dreams? How would you feel if you could fulfill your goals and aspirations? How would you contribute to improving the world?

I understand these are profound questions, but what truly matters are your answers. Your genuine motivations will serve as a thermometer to measure your level of immersion and commitment to your dream. You have the capability to achieve it; all it takes is the decision to start and allow yourself to take the plunge. I am confident that you will succeed.

How to Start a Business?

As mentioned earlier, the first and most crucial step in starting a business is making the decision to embark on the entrepreneurial journey. Begin by assessing your skills, attitudes, talents, and hobbies. Within them, you will find ideas that can help you choose the right business to start. Define your dream in terms of the size of the business you want to establish. Keep in mind that a larger business will require a greater capital investment, so consider your financial resources. Additionally, take into account your availability of time, especially if you have other commitments like being a dependent employee or a student. If you're a beginner, it is advisable to start with a small project.

Planning is essential. Determine your short-term, medium-term, and long-term goals. Assess the resources at your disposal, including financial resources, materials, and others. Develop a plan on how you will execute your ideas and establish a timeline for your activities.

While you may have multiple goals, it is important to fulfill each one step by step, as if you were climbing a staircase, one step at a time. Maintaining motivation throughout your journey is crucial, from the establishment of your business to the achievement of your goals. Expect emotional ups and downs along the way, and staying motivated will help keep your mind clear and focused on carrying out your tasks effectively. Be consistent in your efforts, whether it's taking small steps or making significant strides, but never stop moving forward.

Even though the business is your own idea and dream, it is not healthy to travel this path alone. Build a team that believes in your idea and is committed to the project. Their presence and opinions will keep you aligned with your objectives, maintain your motivation, provide honest feedback, and support you in developing your initiative. Working as a team and delegating responsibilities will enable you to execute your plans in a fresh and objective manner. As a leader, maintain your leadership role by setting an example for your team rather than bossing them around. Control your emotions, be enthusiastic and optimistic, and always exhibit maturity and professionalism. Your team will look to you for guidance, especially during challenging moments.

Often, we have great ideas but struggle to lead and coordinate team actions. No idea can be realized on its own;

it always requires the support of a team that trusts you and believes in your proposals. Being a leader involves both authority and responsibility, which also means managing risks. As the manager of your own business, you will need to make important decisions, sometimes under less than optimal conditions. This requires confidence, determination, and the ability to feel comfortable exercising authority and learning from any mistakes. As mentioned before, this will provide you with valuable experience. It is also crucial to honestly admit mistakes, poorly made decisions, and limitations. Your team will see you as a relatable human being they can trust and believe in.

You are the master of your own destiny. Take the initiative, dare to venture, motivate yourself, be consistent, never stop, continue preparing, learning, and gaining experience. Ultimately, you will achieve what you are building: **STARTING YOUR OWN BUSINESS.**

To begin, you need to have an idea, identify an unsatisfied or partially satisfied need, or simply offer something different or original to fulfill that need. From there, you can establish a business. However, ask yourself: Is this truly what I want to do? Is this something I enjoy? This is the landscape that awaits us, and it's essential to be certain that this is the path you want to traverse.

CONCLUSION

Congratulations on reaching the end of this book! It has been a journey where you have gained a deeper understanding of yourself, identified your skills, experiences, and capabilities. You have also become aware of areas where you excel and areas where you can improve. Recognizing our weaknesses is productive because it allows us to work on them and grow.

Dear reader, this is part of the change you desire. We have traveled from the beginning, exploring what it means to pursue financial and economic independence. We have understood why our world can be seen as both a big business and a jungle. Within yourself, you have found the right reasons to embark on the path of entrepreneurship.

In this book, we have covered the fundamental knowledge needed to start in the business field, always emphasizing the importance of continuously expanding your knowledge with more ideas, processes, and problem-solving methods. We have provided a list of tools that should be at your disposal in the 21st century, enabling you to constantly monitor and evaluate the growth of your business. We have defined these tools and explained how they add value to your entrepreneurial endeavors.

We have discussed the significance of learning and gaining experience, emphasizing the importance of curiosity and a constant thirst for knowledge to enhance our skills. Experience is a result of applying the acquired knowledge, whether it was done correctly or not. In the long run, this experience will turn us into the specialists of tomorrow.

We have shared some of the aptitudes and attitudes that every entrepreneur should possess, understanding that there are many more. The ones covered in this book are just the tip of the iceberg, as there are countless others. It's only a part of the journey. I recommend that you continue reading, improving, and refining yourself. Explore the works of authors like Robert Kiyosaki, Donald Trump, Warren Buffett, among others, and learn from their experiences. Study Jurgen Klaric or Elon Musk and learn from their strategies. Read anything that can help you improve, increase your knowledge, and consequently make better decisions. The more knowledge you possess, the more accurate your decisions will be.

According to some specialists, 60% to 70% of entrepreneurs abandon their businesses within 2 years. Despite these discouraging statistics, it is always more encouraging to take the leap into entrepreneurship than to continue relying on a single source of income.

In conclusion, you have made the decision. This book was created with the intention of showing you what it means to be an entrepreneur and the essential aspects of education, profile, and knowledge required to bring your ideas to life. As mentioned before, the start of this journey begins with the first step—deciding on the business you want to develop. To do that, you need to know yourself, engage in a profitable activity that leverages your strengths, brings you satisfaction, and happiness. When all these aspects are covered, money will likely follow. This is the difference between doing what we love, where money becomes a consequence rather than the ultimate goal.

I believe that the most important aspect of all of this is that you took that first step by reading this book. If you have decided to continue, I estimate that I can continue to assist you. As I mentioned at the beginning, my vision is to provide support, guidance, and learn from people like you. The intention is and will always be to enrich our knowledge and help others in the areas that concern us.

I will continue writing more texts, not only on self-help and personal improvement but also on finance, accounting, administration, and business. I will continue my calling to contribute to those who desire long-awaited financial freedom and foster an entrepreneurial culture.

All of this is aimed at improving your status so that you become a better entrepreneur and transform into a super entrepreneur.

Thank you for allowing me to accompany you on this journey, and I invite you to share your thoughts on this book. Best regards to you.

ABOUT THE AUTHOR

Carlos Cárdenas Verde graduated in Public Accounting from Universidad Nacional Experimental de los Llanos Ezequiel Zamora, Barinas, Venezuela in 2000. With extensive experience as an accountant, financial advisor, and business management consultant, Carlos has devoted much of his career to educating both young people and adults in educational institutions such as the Instituto Universitario de Tecnología Coronel Agustín Codazzi and the Universidad Nacional Experimental Simón Rodríguez.

In addition to his teaching experience, Carlos is recognized for his focus on developing valuable tools for accounting and management information within companies. Through self-taught learning in Digital Marketing and Digital Entrepreneurship, Carlos advocates for teaching accounting as a fundamental pillar for business success and entrepreneurship.

www.ingramcontent.com/pod-product-compliance
Lightning Source LLC
Chambersburg PA
CBHW072019230526
45479CB00008B/292